THE INFLUENCE OF ROME

BUDDHISM, CHRISTIAN AND ISLAM

HTAY LWIN OO

The Influence of Rome
Buddhism, Christian and Islam
Copyright © 2021 by Htay Lwin Oo

Library of Congress Control Number: 2021923823
ISBN-13: Paperback: 978-1-64749-652-4
          ePub: 978-1-64749-653-1

All rights reserved. No part of this publication may be reproduced, distributed, or transmitted in any form or by any means, including photocopying, recording, or other electronic or mechanical methods, without the prior written permission of the publisher or author, except in the case of brief quotations embodied in critical reviews and certain other noncommercial uses permitted by copyright law.

Although every precaution has been taken to verify the accuracy of the information contained herein, the author and publisher assume no responsibility for any errors or omissions. No liability is assumed for damages that may result from the use of information contained within.

Printed in the United States of America

GoToPublish LLC
1-888-337-1724
www.gotopublish.com
info@gotopublish.com

Contents

Preface 1
The influence of the Rome 3
    Still influence 3
    "Son without human father" 4
    "Virgin" 5
Buddhism 6
    The son of God 6
    Sons without fathers' seeds 6
The image of Buddha emerges 1000 years after his death 9
    Most influential anecdote 9
    Wise venerable and scholars do not accept this story 9
    What Buddha taught 11
    The Buddha's Image History 12
    Where the Buddha Image came from 12
    Rome swallowed the Buddhism 14
Christian 16
    What Bible said, "Son of God?" 17
    Mixed Blood Son of God 17
    Man's sperm is essential for women's pregnancy 18
    What is the Holy Spirit? 19
    Filled with Holy Spirit before he was born 19
    Was born because of God's promise 20
    God calls "My son" 20
    Christ 21
    The One 21
    The Son of God 22
    The Son of Man 23

- Descendant of David 23
- From Mary's? Or Joseph's? 23
- Jesus never deniesthat he is son of Joseph 24
- According to Moses' and the prophets' law 24
- Virgin or a young woman? 24
- Some contradicting verses of the Bible 24
- Because of Rome 26

Islam 27
- Wounded Religion 27
- Under the Fatawa (Religious Edict) 27
- Virgin Pure? Or Modest Woman? 27
- No man touched her 28
- *Ruh* 29
- We breathed into her of Our Ruh (21: 91, 66: 12) 29
- According to the Koran, *Ruh* is not needed to exist living thing. 30
- The process of pregnancy 30
- *Ruh* is not Angel nor dignified to Angel 31
- What is *Ruh*? 31
- How Mary got pregnant? 33
- How did the man give the child to her? 34
- Did Allah reveal the verses of Koran carelessly? 35
- A sign to men and mercy from Allah 35
- Many Muslim leaders are not followers of the Koran 37

Citation **38**
- Burmese Books 38
- English 38
- Arabic 38
- Dictionaries 38

Preface

In my knowledge, the religion gives people the noble human moral code and teaches how to attain the intellectual (spiritual) power. But our new generations can not overestimate upon the religion which they believe in under criticizing their illogical myths belief in the multi culture civil society and their social relationship among the different faiths.

Moreover, their scientific educational field of study, they are trying to leave from their obsolete faiths, their traditional myths belief is trying to evict them form their religions. This will lead them two headed way "good and bad".

The good is that they become the revolutionary individual to revolt their minds which are overwhelmed myths and traditional belief so they can create the physical development with logical staff. But they are going to be losing their mind control techniques or how to constraint their bad power of the mind. It is bad thing because their creating the physical development without control bed power of the mind is leading them to establish the suffocated life.

The religious leaders, who are really worried about their followers, are trying to deliver how to get the tranquil mind to reduce their suffocated minds. Their intentions might be good, but they dare not to scrutinize with logical points to own faiths and try to create the story that cover up their myths which already take place their religions.

So they do not become the true helpers to diminish the mind burden of their followers. Their followers receive more burdens of myths plus religions.

As the parable of fire, it is hot, but it gives the lights. The leaders who have good willing on the followers are trying to share the lights cover up the fire with ashes and deliver to them. Their strategies seem to be useful but when in longer and longer the power of the fire is swallowed of with ashes and the followers (the innocent people) are far from knowledge of original fire and its lights.

The brains of the innocent people are full of the ashes, or the strategies of the leaders and their consideration powers are over loaded, and there is no more room to accept the real one.

The brains that full of the over loaded trash needed to be burned to be able to accept the original one. Or clean up the brain's pollutions.

In this book, I present the real teaching of the Holy Books of three religions (Buddhism, Christian and Islam) which against our traditional belief of daily practice or which bewitch our minds.

(1) Buddha teaches not to prayer (prostrate) the Image, but we do every day.

(2) Jesus said he is descendant of King David, but never accept his teaching.

(3) Koran said no human being can be born just half parent, but we against that law for Jesus.

And we are willingly accepting the myths and lure others to follow our indulge minds. We propagate the myths and distribute illogical stories to new generations.

Htay Lwin Oo

The influence of the Rome
Still influence

"When in Rome do as the Romans do" is one of the most well-known proverbs on account to last through history and prove useful for human society.

Today, much of the new generation doesn't know about and aren't interested in Rome. Rome for them is left in ancient stories.

After the 5th century AD, the seeds of the Rome had spread out from its root and came out the many nations in its fruit. Historians have celebrated the final funeral service of Rome one thousand and five hundred years ago.

In this age Rome rests as just a city in the background. It may be said that its strength has diminished, and Rome has been swallowed by a multicultural world. Even today, Romans themselves do as others do under globalization, and it is thought that it has disappeared from the world's political stage.

But we can not say that it has completely left the world, because it owns enough of an invaluable wisdom to know the people's minds. Even though its empire diminished from the political stage of the world, it can build up its banner in the hearts of the people from all over the world to do as Romans when not in Rome.

Its influence in the past had swallowed the world completely before its power was broken. Knowing or not knowing; if Rome is hurt, many people of the world feel pain in their hearts and rise up in anger.

The sophisticated scholars of the Rome were already aware that "religion is the opium of the masses" many years before Karl Marx put it to writing. Roman scholars knew well enough that people would dare not consider their own individual faiths under the fear of heaven and hell.

Romans systematically used those tools to set up their ideology in the people hearts. While accepting other philosophies and religions into their home they could create home-made faiths or traditions and home-made philosophy. Sometimes they gathered others' faith as the raw material and cast these in their own mould to shape it, reproduce it, and distribute it to others.

And in this way, they could dress the world's major religions in their clothes and set up their philosophy within these major religions. Buddhism, Christian and Muslim faiths were like air blown into the same balloon. If the balloon is blowing up, the air inside of it makes more space for it. If the air is released from the balloon, it loses its substance. In other words, Rome could create itself as a God successfully amidst the people's hearts under the names of these religions.

It is indisputable that the more these religions separated and spread through the world, the more Rome's influence overwhelmed the world in the place of God.

"Son without human father"

According to Bible and world history, the Roman Empire's rule and influence stretched into the Middle East, especially Palestine, many years before the birth of Jesus and Christianity's rise as well as in India after Buddha's death. The people from those regions were captivated by Rome's ancient faiths and ideology.

The people of those regions believed that these great men were "sons of God" or "sons of Angel Chief" or "virgins' son" or "were born without fathers' seed."

We can find these kinds of people in a lot of Indian religious histories including Buddhism and Middle Eastern religions.

It may be that these opinions came to Rome from somewhere else, but Rome put it into its mould and exported to others. So, we can say that these opinions came into Buddhism, Christian and Islam from Rome. It is not from any real religion.

We can find that point that the founder of Great Empire, Alexander the Great adopted himself as having mixed blood of Angel Chief; his mother was sired by The Angel Chief, and she gave girth to him. (Guide to the New Testament, p 14)

And the king of Rome Caesar Augustus (BC 27- AD 14) also believed that he himself was the son of the god Apollo; that the god Apollo had assumed the form of a Snake and overwhelmed his mother so that she gave birth to him. (Guide to the New Testament, p 14)

In that era, the world was under the rule of kings who ruled by divine right. Therefore, the religion or philosophy which was the king's belief was also the state religion.

Therefore, the people of those regions' beliefs were practiced enough in a belief system where the Great men were sons of god that it was naturally their opinion that it was so. They did not consider whether it was myth or real, nor did they interest themselves in logical answers.

"Virgin"

In the minds of the people of those regions, was the belief that the holy woman must be a pure virgin, that no man had touched her in a sexual relationship in her whole life. They thought that if a woman had sexual relationship with a man, either legal or illegal, she was not pure.

First, they want to portray the great man or character of their myth as born by holy woman; on the other hand, they want their holy woman to be a pure virgin even though she delivered a son. So, they need to invent many fabrications to create the scenario where their holy woman was a pure virgin and a mother.

The opinion "virgin" did not come from any religion because every religion allowed legal marriage. and no religion says that the legal married woman is unchaste. Within a woman or man, any human being's holiness is dependant on his/her morals or guarding against evil. In this scenario a "virgin" is not the only holy woman/ man in any religion.

We can find that there is the opinion "virgin" in Rome's religion or philosophy. They believed in "vestal virgins" in their religion.

Buddhism

Most of the non-Buddhist world thinks that Buddhism exists itself in Asia and it may be one branch of Hindu. We can make the argument that Rome's influence played a large part in shaping Buddhist belief systems and ways of practice and in some ways swallowed Buddhism completely.

The son of God

The idea of a "son of God" is introduced into Buddhism is at some stage of its development. It is uniformly thought that Buddhism and Christianity are not the same at all, yet somewhere in Buddhist belief; the monks began to be referred to as sons of God.

But somewhere in Buddhist philosophy, the father is likened to a god and mother of Buddha a virgin. That the monks are called "sons of God" does not mean that they were born and sired by God. And mothers of the monks are not virgins who delivered the child without a human male seed. They are successors of the religious heritage of Gotama Buddha whom they believed as God, so they are called as "sons of God." Even though the opinions are very different in Christianity, the usage "son of God" came into Buddhism from Rome and not from their own religious teaching. In the scriptures written from Buddha's words through the experience of the monks, Buddha never calls the monks "My sons." Even His own son "**Rahula**" was not called My Son when he became a monk. Buddha used the monks by name or as "My venerable."

Sons without fathers' seeds

We can find many myths in Buddhist religious history wherein people were born without a fathers' seed. The most famous event is of *Suwanna Sama*, the story of "one who returned to life with a gold pot to be seen by his blind parents". In his story, he was born without father's seed as his father did not have a sexual relationship with his mother. In this story, it was by rubbing her navel with his finger that she became pregnant.

We can also find another story like this in the history of Buddha. His mother *Ma-ya* was barren, and in her old age. His father King *Sodsawdana* let her sleep in a separate room, and an Angel spoke to her in a dream about her child. The Angel said that the holy white elephant would open her ribs and dwell in her womb, making her pregnant with her child (Gotama).

Why do these stories portray these persons to be born without a fathers' seed? The answer is very clear. Rome's influence not only stretched into their land but into their stories and myths as well. From the interface with the Roman culture, the mothers of these people became virgin receptacles of divine conception as pure or holy women. They either innovated from Roman influence, or Roman influence overwhelmed them. In this case, the virgin birth incorporated itself into the story of Buddha's coming into being.

But these ideas of "son of God" and "sons- without fathers' seeds" are not very successful in inspiring one to Buddhism. These are still rare because whatever is said in their religious stories, Buddhist believe that the king *Sodsawdana* is real father of Prince Siddartha who became Buddha Gotama.

While Rome's influence was not always successful in inspiring their stories and faiths into Buddhism, their biggest success in effecting Buddhist belief and practice is when the first image of Buddha was rendered from sculpture and imagery of the Roman god Apollo bearing the Buddha's name.

There are many beautiful teachings and speeches relevant to our human society in Buddhism, but many of the religious scholars (*Dama Saria*) and many of monks are persuading their followers to adore the pagoda, stupa, or representation of Buddha (the thing which is built up to worship), rather than to follow the human moral codes of Buddha's teaching. This means that they are urging their followers to follow the influence of Rome rather than the original doctrines of Buddha.

In very recent years, the world Buddhist community erupted in anger toward Hollywood because of a film entitled Hollywood Buddha in which the advertising for the film contains a picture of the actor sitting on top of the Buddha Image (idol). Some countries with a religiously Buddhist majority, such as Thailand, complained about Hollywood's usage of this imagery.

In another instance, the world Buddhist community burst out in their anger upon the Taliban when its regime destroyed the ancient Buddha Images in Afghanistan.

Their cause of anger and complaint is based on the love and admiration that they have for the Buddha. (Yet their anger is derived from their attachment to Buddha's image or idol) They are not guilty because of anger and complaint about the insulters. They love their Buddha Image, they pray (pay homage) before It. In their mind they admire the Buddha image so much that there is no way to evaluate its value in their hearts. Almost every Buddhist of the world makes a shrine/shelf (admirable place) for it in their houses. When their adorable thing is insulted, who can patient?

They heartily believe that it is really Image of their God (Buddha) that has been defiled. Their hearts have clung to this image. They love it and if some one insults it or seems to insult it, intentionally or unintentionally, they can not calm down their minds.

The image of Buddha emerges 1000 years after his death

Most influential anecdote

Most Buddhists accept that the Buddha Image was made with the permission of Buddha Gotama himself based on stories written later. According to these stories, in the era of Buddha's life, He traveled to an Angelic Place (Tusita) to preach for his mother, (in the persona of a virgin or angel) who died when she gave birth to him. The king *Pasaynadi Kosala* who very much admired him and wanted to remember to him during his absence, made Buddha's Image with Santaku wood and made a prayer to it. When Buddha came back to world, the Image was standing and saluting to Buddha. Buddha said to it "You Image, be easy, you are going to be here on my behalf, after me for the four kinds of (human and) animals." According to this story, later generations of Buddhists copied that original image or used it for a template for sculpture (idol), to continue worship of Buddha in this way.

If this story were true, who can deny the acceptance that this image is really Buddha's Image?

We should consider where this story came from to Buddhism because there is not any mention of these events in the Pali Pitakat (main Buddhist scripture or teaching of Buddha Gotama).

Wise venerable and scholars do not accept this story

The well-known Burmese Second Monywe Sayadaw venerable Ahdatesaranthi (1766-1834) said that that story came from the Vedinkuli Yaza drama. It was neither included in the 550 Jatak's (Buddha's life stories) nor accounted for in books of written from convening the Buddha synod (*Sankha Yana*). The stories themselves came from the Roman influence in the form of plays from Yome (Burmese's accent Y for R). This is why the *Sankhas* (Monks) do not hold it in esteem as truth. (Myatminglar Buddhism religious journal, Burmese Language, Dec '93, P 50, 51)

Some scholars say that Yome refers not to Rome but to Yodaya (Thailand), The Burmese word for Thailand is Yodaya because Ayoddeya was the last capital of its kingdom occupied by Burmese.

In the research of the Cleric (Sayadaw), it is impossible for Yome to be Thailand (Yodoya), because the Buddha Image entered into the Buddhism world not from Yodaya (Thailand) but from Rome. Burmese word for Rome is Yorma (Yome). On the other words, the Buddha Images was flowing into the Buddhism world from West to East, not from East to West. (See The Buddha's image history)

Tike Soe, a Buddhist scholar of Burma (Myanmar), a strong Buddhist country, confessed in the Myatmingalar (a well-known religious journal), that the disciples of the Buddha Gotama accepted that Buddha is *Ahseintaya. Ah pamayya* means there is no formidable (parable) like Buddha in the world. Buddha cannot be duplicated. Therefore almost 1000 years after Buddha death, they still had not made any Image of Buddha.

He also gives good proof of this in the search for Buddha's image at the pinnacle of *Sanshi*, built by King Ahthoka (Asoka) in central India (BC 3-1 century). The figures at this place (in relief) depict the story of an escape from his father's temple as Prince Seiddahta (Buddha Gotama's young name) went into forest to look for Dhama (universal truth). The story shows a relief of the horse Kandaka, (Prince Seiddahta's riding horse), and a relief of the Angel who quieted the sound of the horses' footsteps through the palace, lending to the prince's escape. In the events of this relief story, among these statues, there is no relief of Buddha (Seiddahta). While no image of Buddha was found here, what was found were reliefs of Prince Seiddahta footsteps.

Not far from there, in the carved stone letters of Barahote (BC 200), there are relief of the Bodi, (banyan tree under which Buddha took to a practice of meditation to attain his omniscience intelligent power or enlightenment), and a relief of an altar, but no relief (image) of Buddha. (Myatminglar Buddhism religious journal, Burmese Language, Dec '93, P 50, 51)

We should heed this document. The disciples of Buddha and his foremost followers did see the Buddha while he was still alive, and they would have the best knowledge of the appearance of Buddha Gotama. If they made a Buddha Image, it would be an accurate image of Buddha's appearance. Yet they did not carve an image. Why did they not set Buddha's image into stone? Did they not have love of him, Or want to admire him?

In reality, they had much love and admiration for their teacher Buddha Gotama. They followed the real teachings of Buddha as best they could, and they tried to set themselves up in a good practice of Buddhism.

What Buddha taught

In the Pitakat (the Buddhist scripture), Buddha taught against a person cult of worship aimed toward him as an individual. We can get this teaching from Apadana Pali II.

"buddha ruphayatein Utar tada allvedi mun zinor, allan Vakkali keinrupay ramasay balananditay"

"As Buddha knew that I took pleasure in worshiping him or obsessed to Budda's image (appearance) so I was admonished" (by Buddha) "Vekkali, don't do that, why are you obsessing on the image (my appearance) that is obsessed by the stupid (uneducated) people." (Vekkali Htayra Apadana 53)

"yor hi pasadi saddammun samun pasadi panditor, appasamarnor saddamun mun pasampi na pasadi"

"Those who are wise see the moral principles (sermon), it means he sees me; if he does not see the moral principle (sermon), it means he can not see me even though he sees me." (Vekkali Htayra Apadana 54)

"anandavenawor Kayor vesa mokekhasa mupamor arwarsorsava rogarnan ponezor dokekhasa kaywalor"

"Image is measured, has sins, the parable of poison of tree, the place of all diseases, the pile of all poverties." (Vekkali Htayra Apadana 55)

In Sutta (verse) 55, Buddha refers to himself for his physical not for spiritual. All these verses are very beautiful and admonish his followers not to obsess on the image, but to do good practice under the natural law (Dhama).

He taught that the Dhama (Admonish or to do good practice or meditation) is the most important thing being the main root of the religion. A personal cult is vain for religion. Any person who approaches him for a personal cult is ignorant. But today, we can see what Buddhist's are doing clearly. Wherever they reside, they try to build up the so-called Buddha Image (idols).

Another point said in Khodedaka Pahta of Pali Pitakat about wrong belief is…

"bahome way saranan yanti pabbatani wanarni sa, ahrama rokkha zaytrani manusa bayatazzita"

"As from fear and danger, many people worship (pray to) <u>the thing built up for prayer,</u> like hills, forests, monasteries (temples) and their adorable trees.

"netan kho saranan khayman netan sarana motetaman, netan sarana mar gamma sava dokekha pa motzsati"

"Like this, the worship or belief is not saving one from danger (hell), like this, it is not a noble belief, like this, worship or faith cannot save one from all kinds of sufferings. *(Damah Pada 188-189)*

From the verse 188 the word *zaytrani* refers to *Zayti*. Some scholars translate it to pagoda, but the Pali word *Zayti* is derived from *Zaytiya* which means "build up to (worship) prayer." This word is very broad, but very clear to understand. Anything which is built up for (worship) prayer is *Zaytiya* (*Zayti*)

And then another word *ahrama,* refers to not only monastery, but to all the things belonging to monastery's compound.

In the Buddhism scripture, the word "stupid" and "not safe from danger" are synonymous and are used by Buddha Gottama, chastising his followers to avoid personal cult worship of himself or to an image (build up to prayer). And there is no verse contradicting these admonishments in the Pali Pitakat.

The Buddha's Image History

Where the Buddha Image came from

The people, if they love, like or admire a person, will take a picture, painting, relief, statute or photo to remember him/ her, which is not sin.

But in any religion, the good followers need to heed their teacher (Buddha, Jesus or Mohammad). Otherwise, the myths and anecdotes are rush into the mix and the real religion becomes unpurified.

THE INFLUENCE OF ROME

(1200 years After Buddha's death) About AD 7th century, crowned Images were starting to make in appearances in the Bengal and Bihar states of India. These Images also flowed into Burma, Lao, Thailand, and Cambodia (From West to East). These are not real images of Buddha; these were the basic images (the first Buddha images) from Gandara (Afghanistan). *(Yangon Distance University 2000 annual magazine, Burmese Language, P 50)*

We need to follow the pathways of Buddhism to reach the first Buddha image and find out where it came from. Gandara (Afghanistan) was overwhelmed by the influence of Alexander the Great of the Greeks, and the people of Gandara (Afghanistan) were the shadowed by Rome's influence. When these people accepted Buddhism, they made a sample of the Greek/Roman god Apollo and sculpted the Buddha Image with the god Apollo's face, body and manner, but with the thick cloth of the Buddhist monks robe from the *Gantara* region (now Afghanistan). That was in about AD 5th century under the era of king Kanashaka. (Myatminglar Buddhism religious journal, Burmese Language, Jan '94, P 55)

The King Ahthoka (Asoke), known very well in Buddhist history, for the propagation of Buddhism into his Moriya Empire. According to this record, under the era of King Ahthoka, (a main distributor of Buddhism) that even he did not make any Image of Buddha. But, later, under the King Kanashak's dynasty, the Image started to rise; actually, it was not an image of the real Buddha; it was the image of the god Apollo.

Note: In 2001, in reality, the Taliban regime destroyed the Image of god Apollo, which had been built un but people of the world thought that it was the image of Buddha because it was named Buddha for very long time.

The Buddhist world has been betrayed, passing through many generations with the belief that the image of the Buddha that they revered was of their beloved teacher, when in actuality it was an image of the god Apollo. The fake has existed as reality in their hearts.

Today, most Buddhist's believe that the Image of Buddha is real, and they love it much. They use much money, wealth, and jewelry to make and remake it. Amazingly we can find the Rome and Greek god Apollo image today is almost the same as the Buddha Image. We can clearly see this.

The in-destructible evidence and proof of this is the Image of Apollo from a French museum that was about 90 percent the same today as Buddha's Image.

Apollo (Apollon), c. 600 BCE

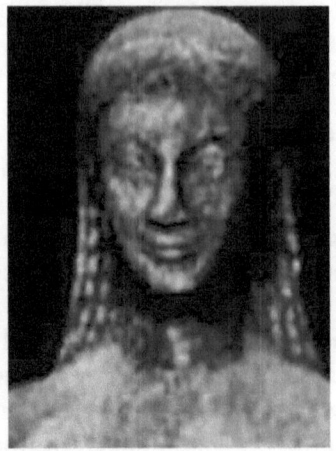
Apollo of Melos

One of the Buddha Images

Rome swallowed the Buddhism

From this we can see that the Buddhism of today has been altered greatly by Roman influence, from the stories which contradict the scriptures, the lack of imagery of Buddha in ancient temple sites, and the resemblance of modern images of the Buddha to the Hellenistic images of the god Apollo of Rome.

Some practitioners try to dispute this by saying that they build up the Buddha image as a symbol, not for worship. But these kinds of books and opinions are very rare among the Buddhist thought. There are many books about the thirty-two signs of the holy male (Maha Pu Ri Sa) that compose the Buddha Image.

Mostly Buddhists follow these kinds of myths and not the real teaching of Buddha. Many Buddhist scholars and monks (Buddhism's spoken persons) are talking about their Buddha for cult idolatry rather than the real teachings. In the other words, they use their time to propagate the god Apollo's image under the name of Buddha rather than the vehicle of his teachings for enlightenment.

Rome has already taken a position in the Buddhists of the world's hearts. Who can extract the truth from the myth? By this way, Rome will be alive in the Buddhist home for ever.

Christian

Rome Enter into Christian

Romans failed to change Buddhism with the "the idea of God" and "virgin" but they were successful in transforming the Apollo Image into Buddha. According to the Bible, Christianity is different from Buddhism, it does not accept the practice of idol worship, but the God in whom they believe in is almost the same Angel Chief (Isaiah 19:1). With a physical body, almost the same as the image of the god Apollo. So, they can dye Christianity with their belief easily. It can be said that Christianity is the most influenced by Rome amidst the world religions. The Christian belief that "Jesus is son of God" was innovated from the founder of Great Empire, Alexander the Great, who adopted himself as mixed blood of an Angel Chief; his mother was also sired by The Angle Chef, and she gave birth to him. (Guide to the New Testament, p 14)

And the king of Rome Caesar Augustus (BC 27- AD 14) also believed himself to be a son of the god Apollo; the god Apollo assumed the form of a Snake and overwhelmed his mother that she gave birth to him. (Guide to the New Testament, p 14)

The Christian propagandas (crusaders) used to visit to our home, preach about Christianity, and invite the people to convert to their sect. They have good will for people, and they want people to be able to escape from hell. They believe that all people of the world were born with sin because of Adam and Eve's (the parents of all human beings of the world) transgression in the garden (original sin). The parents of human race sinned in the garden (paradise) and that is why the God punished them and sent into the world.

The crusaders said that "every single religion is good, but Christianity is better because the sinners can absolve themselves of original sin through the belief that Jesus is Son of God. Jesus does atonement for all kinds of sins of the human being. Even though there are better verses for the human societies in the Bible, most of the crusaders omit these beautiful verses and stay intent upon their well-trained words, which is the Rome's ideology and not Jesus' teaching.

We should not ignore their good will and their sacrifice for the people. But a faith in the cover of the book cannot reach the truth or the real teachings of Jesus as a descendant of King David.

What Bible said, "Son of God?"

The words "son of God" when used in the Bible is not the same ideology of Rome's myths. We can clearly find out this ideology in following verses.

Who are the 'sons of God'? Many Bible passages refer to this specifically. Here are three of them that standout.

>(i)—everyone who does what is right is God's son.

>(ii) Blessed are the peacemakers, for they shall be called sons of God.

>(iii)For all who are led by the Spirit of God are sons of God.

Every Christian understands that the meanings of the passages mentioned above are the "**honor of the God**". Not a literal translation of being sired by God, and not like the Roman belief of son of Apollo. All the people of mentioned above were born naturally from the natural union of a father and mother. But according of the crusaders, Christian clerics', Jesus was different from them.

Mixed Blood Son of God

The crusaders said that Jesus is the son of God not because of his qualification or honor, but because he is really son of God. A man born without having a human father by his mother Mary delivered by God (some said sired by God). They cite the following verses.

(i)When his mother Mary had been betrothed to Joseph, before they came together, she was found to be with child of Holy Spirit. (Matt 1: 18)

(ii)But he had no sexual relations with her before she gave birth to her son. (Matt 1: 25)

(iii)A voice said from the cloud "This is my son,---" (Luke 9: 35)

(iv)Jesus is the Messiah (Matt 16: 16, John 1: 40, 41)

(v)The father and I are one. (John 10: 30)

(vi)Jesus is son of God. (Matt 14: 33)

And so on, too many verses are cited when they explain this to the people. If we listen to their explanation without perusing the Bible, we should accept that Jesus is mixed blood Son of God, a man without a human father.

Before these verses are considered, we need to figure out from where this philosophy came into Christianity and why they give these verses to use as mortar for hold together their philosophy.

If we look to the followers of Jesus, they believed that Jesus was a Great Man and a master of the kingdom of heaven. And the God whom they believe is almost same the Angel or Angel Chief as the Roman image of gods. We can pull out this idea from the Bible. "The Lord is coming to Egypt, riding swiftly on a cloud." (Isaiah 19: 1)

On the other hand, many years before Jesus was born, the region where he was born had been under the Roman Empire. So, under the logical points, no one can deny that the people of that region's interpreted the birth of Jesus is clouded by Roman influence.

Therefore, it can be strongly said that the story that Jesus is the mixed blood son of God, is coming from Rome's influence not from the Bible because Bible said that-

Man's sperm is essential for women's pregnancy

The Bible states that the natural law of birth requires a man's seed (sperm) for pregnancy. It gives proof in the story of Lot and his daughter (Genesis 19: 30-38). In this story, women needed the man's sperm for pregnancy. The daughters had sexual relations with their own father Lot. Lot was not an ordinary man; he was a prophet of God. If God wanted to break His natural law which had been already prescribed, He could. But He proves that He never broke His promise and His laws. That's why He allowed what the daughters did with their own father.

According to Bible, Mary was neither an angel nor a virgin for the whole of her life. She was like other women of the world, and she also needed the man's sperm for Joseph's children, Simon and Judas (Matt 13: 55). If this were so, why would we want to follow the Rome's faith for the anointed one Jesus?

Even the natural law which is mentioned above is contained in Bible clearly. Crusaders use the verse Matt 1: 20 "For it is by the Holy Spirit that she was conceived" as one of their citations for favor to Rome. By this citation, some may think that Holy Spirit is sperm or like sperm because of they thought that it can make Mary pregnant. But we can strongly affirm that the Holy Spirit is not the sperm. What the Bible contains about Spirit as Spirit, Holy Spirit, God's Spirit and Spirit of Lord occurs about 260 times but doesn't refer to sperm anywhere. No woman can get pregnant this way because of the laws of nature, or laws of God. That is why, there is no reason that the Holy Spirit can be on behalf of the Human Male' sperm, in regard to Mary's pregnancy.

If this is so,

What is the Holy Spirit?

We can figure out that the Holy Spirit refers to the word of God (which means the intellect power or revelation or omen). The Bible itself said about this point in the following verses.

> (i)" The Spirit of the Lord will give him **wisdom, and knowledge and skill to rule** his people" (Isaiah 11: 2)
>
> (ii)--and **the word of God** is the sword which the Spirit gives you. (Ephesians 6:17)

These two points very clearly support other verses of the Bible pertaining to this issue.

According to the Bible, not only Mary, but also John's father Zechariah and Jesus were given the Holy Spirit. (Luke 1: 67, 2: 25)

Every crusader accepts that the Holy Spirit that is given to Zechariah and Jesus is the wisdom or knowledge or intellect or omen. But the same word "the Holy Spirit" is given to Mary as a means of conception. Why?

If we want to believe that Mary became pregnant without a human male's sperm, our idea is then becoming not only to follow the myth instead of natural law of Bible, but also wishing her to be worthy of death because bible said women or men who changed the natural process into that which is against nature are worthy of death (Romans 1: 26- 32).

Filled with Holy Spirit before he was born

Some crusaders said that even though the Holy Spirit inspired Zechariah, the authors of the Bible, Matthew, Luke, Mark, John and others, were somehow different in their interpretation of the story of

Mary. She was given it (the Holy Spirit) before she delivered her child (Jesus), and Jesus was filled with the Holy Spirit before he was born. She did not need to have the human male's sperm to become pregnant and she got pregnant by the Holy Spirit, so Jesus did not have human father and he is the son of God. This is another reason relaying the bias of Rome. We can accept their words "Jesus was filled with the Holy Spirit before he was born," but we have to consider their drawing the conclusion "so he is the son of the God" because the Bible said even though he was a person filled with the Holy Spirit before he was born, he had to have a human father. We can get this point from (Luke 1: 15). John was filled with the Holy Spirit before he was born, but every crusader accepts that John is not the son of God, nor that his mother Elisabeth was a virgin. That was law of nature and Bible does not break the law of nature.

Was born because of God's promise

Some try to counter that Jesus was born because of God's promise and God's Spirit. That is why his birth was different from the birth of John and he is really son of God, not because of being honored by the Holy Spirit. This poses the question of why they don't believe that Sara, one of the wives of Abraham was virgin while her son Isaac was considered "Son of God." The Bible clearly says that Isaac was born because of God's promise (Galatians 4; 23) and because of God's Spirit (Galatians 4: 29). While the Bible honors this person, it doesn't change the story of his birth to counter the law of nature, and so nobody denies it. If we insist on breaking the natural law, we would be followers of Rome's myths and not followers of the Bible.

God calls "My son"

The Christian propagandas say that even though Isaac was born because of God's promise and God's Spirit, God does not call him "My son." In this they cannot accept that Isaac was the son of God. With Jesus on the other hand, God calls Jesus as My Son (Luke 9: 36), leading to the strong belief that Jesus really is the Son of God and that he does not have a human father. We cannot be upset with any one's belief as everyone has the right to their beliefs, but we should consider why these people do not believe that Israel and David were Sons of God nor their mothers as virgins? Because God said, "Israel is my son, even my firstborn" (Exodus 4:22) and "You (David) are my son" (Psalm 2: 7). If we follow the real teachings and logical points of the

Bible, we should accept the conclusion of that same Bible theory. Even the Bible says that Israel and David are called "My Son", they were born by natural law by their fathers and mothers, not only because of only their mothers.

Christ

The pro- Rome propagandas never give up their ideas and looked for many reasons to confirm that Jesus was born without father's seed. They said that Jesus is Christ is not an ordinary one, he is the Christ (Matt 16:16, John 1:40-41). He does not need a human father to come into the world.

Whatever they believe is their own rights, but we should defend for the natural law of Bible. According to the Bible, that Christ does not mean the Virgin's son or Son of God is very clear. It is the Greek word for Hebrew "Messiah", and it means "the anointed one." (Good News Bible, today English Version, 1976, P 326)

In the Bible, Cyrus (Isaiah 45: 1), the priest (Leviticus 4:3) and David (Psalm 2:2) are the anointed ones (Holy Bible, King James Version). That David is Christ is found directly in Psalm 2:2 of the Holy Bible translated into the Burmese by Rev. A. Judson, D.D.

But no one believes that Cyrus, the priest, and David are Sons of God, and their mothers are Virgins in the way that they believe that Jesus is. Why do they want people to believe that just Jesus is the Son of God and that his mother is Virgin?

The One

In the highest degree, they want people to believe that Jesus is not only Son of God but also that he is God himself because of saying that "the Father and I are One" (John 10:30).

How does this idea of the One become the belief of Jesus as the Son of God or God? The Bible never mentions that the One is the Son of God or God. Jesus He Himself solves this question of the meaning of "Son of God" when he said that those who are chosen by God and sent into the world are "Son of God" (John 10: 36). He was not saying that he was a son of God or God because of being sired by God. Why would they want to neglect the words of Jesus?

"The One" is the highest degree and example of belief and trust not to be concerned about the physical body's existence. We can find one point in the Bible is "I in them (those who believe in Jesus) and you in me, so that they may be completely one," (John 17:23). This verse says clearly that the spiritual conditions of believers and Jesus and God are one. This does not mean the believers and Jesus and God are same, nor that the believers are sons of God or their mothers virgins.

And one more verse we can find in the Bible is "For we are members of his body, of his flesh, and of his bones" (Ephesians 5:30). In this verse we refer to Paul and Ephesians their reference to Jesus. But no one accepts that Paul and Ephesians are the body of Jesus.

The Son of God

The Bible uses about 48 times the phrase "Son of God." (It is difficult to say exactly how many times because of different manuscripts of the Bible). But Jesus He Himself did not say that He is the Son of God because of being Sired by God, or being Virgin's Son, or from not having a Human father.

Although He himself used the word "Son" **2 times** in John 5:19, 27, but he said, "the Son of Man," (man being one born of father and mother) not "the Son of God" (John 5: 27).

And Jesus said he is Son of God **2 times** in John 10: 34-36, but when he mentions the Son of God it is with the meaning that those who are chosen by God and send into the world, not the son in a literal sense of being born because of being sired by God or God (John 10: 36).

God calls Jesus "My son" **3 times** in Mark 3: 17, 17:5 and Luke 9:35, but God calls Israel in the same way in Exodus 4:22 and David in Psalm 2: 7.

The **29 times** in The Acts, Romans, Corinthians, Galatians, Ephesians, Thessalonians, Hebrew, and Letters of John and, **6 times** in Matt 14:33, 16:16, Mark 1:1, John 1: 34, 49, 11:27. That this phrase is written have been used by followers of Jesus to create, through their interpretation, a personal cult of Jesus. That they didn't believe in Jesus heartily as really the "Son of God" is pointed out in Mark 14: 50. "Then all the disciples left him and ran away."

The other **6 times** where this phrase was used in the Bible, it was used by unbelievers to mock Jesus.

Overall, none of the phrase "Son of God" from the Bible mentions Virgin's Son or that Jesus was born without human father.

The Son of Man

The Holy Bible never says that Jesus came to the world as God being, but Bible just says he came to the world as human being (I John 4: 2, 3, II John 1:7) and Jesus He Himself said "Son of Man" over **70 times** in the Bible. How then, do people believe that Jesus' father was God rather than man?

Descendant of David

The Bible strongly says that Jesus is the descendant of David (Romans 1:3, Revelation 22:16, Luke 1: 32. And every single follower of the Bible accepts that Jesus is descendant of David.

If so, we should consider from which side Jesus relate to David? From Mary's or From Joseph's?

From Mary's? Or Joseph's?

The Bible contains the name Mary mother of Jesus about 32 times, but nowhere is it said that Mary is from the line of David.

Even though in Matt 1:23 the mother of Emmanuel is Mary, when we study about the mother of Emmanuel in Isaiah, it said the speaker is Isaiah and listeners are the descendants of David, but it did not say that Mother of Emmanuel is the descendant of David (Isaiah 7:13-14). And there is no document in Bible that Mary is the descendant of King David.

If this were so, how is Jesus related to King David?

According to the Bible, Jesus' connection to David is through Joseph, because the Bible itself affirms that Joseph is the descendant of King David. (Matt 1:20, Luke 1:27, 2:4 and generation list of Matt 1: 1-16, Luke 3: 23-31)

That if he were not born of Joseph, he could not be called the descendant of David is clear.

Jesus never denies that he is son of Joseph

The people who know his parents and family say before him "he is Joseph's son," (Matt 13:55, 56, Luke 4:22 and John 6:42) but he never denies it. Why he was silent? Silent means admit. He is righteous man, he dared to die for truth, he never lied the people, he never betrayed the people, if he were not the son of Joseph, he would deny it when he was called "son of Joseph."

According to Moses' and the prophets' law

And, according to Moses and the prophets' law, Jesus is really son of Joseph, not stepson of Joseph. –Philip found Nathanael and told him "We have found the one whom Moses wrote about in the book of the law and whom the prophets also wrote about. He is Jesus, son of Joseph, from Nazareth." (John 1: 45)

Virgin or a young woman?

Matt 1: 23 said that mother of Immanuel is Virgin, but the Isaiah 7: 24 said the mother of Immanuel is a young woman (Good News Bible explains in its food note that Hebrew word here translated "young woman" is not the specific term for "virgin" but refers to any young woman of marriageable age.) The original Hebrew word means a young woman and not virgin in the way that we use the word.

Some contradicting verses of the Bible

When the Bible is studied, some contradicting verses are found which are not said by God or Angel or Jesus, that try to annul the strong verses that are said by God or Angel or Jesus and the entire law of the Bible.

For Example, "But he (Joseph) had no sexual relations with her (Mary) before she gave birth her son (Jesus)" (Matt 1: 25). When this verse is considered, it is not connected with a former verse from Matt 1: 24 "So when Joseph woke up, he married Mary, as the angel of the Lord had told him to do".

Did Joseph do sexual relation with Mary or not, who can know without an account by Joseph or Mary? In the Bible, Joseph nor Mary ever admit that they did not have sexual relations with each other before Jesus was born.

And we consider the verse Matt 1:25, the God or Angel or Jesus did not say these words. If so, who said these words?

These words are spoken anonymously, or the speaker is hidden. These words not only annul the words of Jesus "I am descended from the family of David", the words of Angel "Joseph, descendant of David," and the words of those who they knew him from the Nazareth "isn't he the son of Joseph?" but also cancel the entire theory outlined in the Bible that a human cannot be delivered without human male's sperm (Genesis 19: 30-38).

And another verse from the Bible "He was the son, so people thought, of Joseph," (Luke 3: 23) should be considered. This verse means that Jesus is not really son of Joseph because of the words "so people thought." If this were so, how can Jesus (Emmanuel) be a descendant of David according to the Bible? On the other hand, many of the translations, including King James Version, write the words "so people thought" in parenthesis (-).

Why do the other translators omit the parenthesis? It is understood that the words inside the bracket and without the bracket are very different.

That the words inside the bracket are explanations or additions which are not contained in the original is generally understood. The Good News Bible simply admits in its foot notes that many verses and words of the Bible had been added later.[1]

Who can say that the words "so people thought" and "he had no sexual relation with her before Jesus was born" are not added into Bible later? If we accept these two sentences, we have to throw away the entire law of the Bible and the true teachings of Jesus. Thus, believing Jesus is to be a character of Myth, and not is a real human being.

But most of the crusaders (spokespersons of Christianity) are talking about Matt 1:25 and the words from Luke 3:23 "so people thought" and try to cover up the whole Bible with these two verses. They dare to ignore the whole Bible and they are enraptured themselves within these two verses. Why?

---

[1] Good News Bible, The British & Foreign Bible Society 146 Queen Victoria St, London EC4V 4BX © American Bible Society 1976

Because of Rome

The answer is clear, that the Rome's influence had already rooted into their trust.

In this way, Rome is alive for ever in the Christians' faith and practice too.

Islam

Wounded Religion

Islam is the religion most wounded by the Rome's myths. The whole religion is under the **fatawa** (religious edict) sentenced by the sign of the last day, Imam Mahdi (The last hiding Imam, the Quran never speaks of him), Jesus, Mary, Darja (One eye man, the Koran never speaks of him) and many verbally transmitted stories.

Even though Muslims who believe in Islamic faith boast that they accept monotheism, and that Muhammad is the messenger of Almighty God and the last Prophet, there is intensely internal fighting concerning Jesus, because of their similar Christian beliefs shadowed by Rome's influence. They never argue with each other about the Prophet Muhammad and how he was born and how he passed away or about others except Jesus.

Under the Fatawa (Religious Edict)

If those who disbelieve that Jesus was born by the Virgin Mother, he is not Muslim according to the regulation of the world's largest Islamic organization, *Olamah* (Religious Educated Organization). Their well-trained Muslim leaders peach to the followers elaborately and eloquently in an organized way that Mary (mother of Jesus) is Virgin Pure, *Ah Sanat Fa r Jaha* that no man has touched her, and that the Angel comes and embraces her, so she becomes pregnant.

And strengthen their idea, they exaggerate about the mystic power of Jesus that he was born because of ***Ruh***, and that he can speak to the people from the time when he was a baby in the cradle, and that he can bring the dead to life, and many others.

All those ideas had sunk in from Rome's ancient beliefs and they are neither from the Holy Koran nor is the Prophet Muhammad teaching.

Virgin Pure? Or Modest Woman?

The well-trained Muslim preachers used to speak that Mary is Virgin Pure *Ah Sanat Fa ra Jaha* so their followers believe that Mary, is mother only to Jesus for her whole life because the Koran never mentions about her other children by name. However, according to the Holy Koran the word *Ah Sanat Fa ra Jaha* does not contain the meaning "Virgin Pure". Muslim people are not aware of this because of their lack of understanding of the Koran and dare not to think beyond their pioneers (Maddarasas).

When the T the phrase *Ah Sanat Fa r Jaha* is perused, there are two words contained in it and the first word *Ah Sanat* comes from *Hasana* It means pure from illegal sexual intercourse or avoidance from adultery. It does not mean Virgin Pure. The Holy Koran clearly says that *Muho Sanato* legally married women (4:24) and legally divorced women (4:24, 5:5), experience legal sexual relationships, but they avoid the illegal sexual intercourse of adultery (24:4).

The Holy Koran never says that *Ah Sanat* is Virgin Pure *Ab karam* the Koran uses its specified term for Virgin Pure is *Ab karam* (56: 36, 66: 5) not the word *Hasana*, if so why do these preachers try to translate the word *Hasana* Virgin Pure only for Mary?

And then another word *Fa ra Jaha* that is contained in the phrase of *Ah Sanat Fa ra Jaha* comes from *Foe ruj* which means "rift or sexual organ", when the two words in combination mean "She avoids her sexual organ from illegal sexual intercourse," not avoid from the legal marriage or legal sexual relationship.

No man touched her

These preachers cite the words of Mary "no man touched me *Lam yam sasani Bashar*" to strengthen their bewitched idea and exaggerate that Mary never married or was touched by a man in her whole life.

When the Holy Koran is studied thoroughly and fully understood, we can find that the Koran contains these words two times. The first time is-

When the Angle came to her and sent the news about her child, she said "How shall I have a baby, no man has touched me yet." (3: 47) and

When a messenger came and said to her that he would give a pure son to her, she said "how shall I have a son, no man has touched me yet; I am not unchaste," (19:20).

According to the Koran, the words *"Lam yam sasani Bashar"* just means "no man has touched me yet (to get the child)" and not that she won't be touched by any male in her whole life (to get the child).

When we consider these words; ***Lam yam sasani Bashar***" there are three words contained in it. First the interrogative word ***Lam*** which means negative for past to present, (If the interrogative word ***Lan*** was used, it would refuse from present to future).

And the word ***Massas*** means "touched, has the sexual intercourse" and ***Bashar*** is man not Angel.

When she heard the news (which was not a pregnancy) about her child, she had not been touched by any male, understanding, and acknowledging the natural law that in order to have a child; she would need to be touched by male.

The news was only the message, not the thing necessary for immediate pregnancy, meaning that she is going to have a child in future through natural means and not right now.

When she got the message, she had not been touched yet by any man, nor had she yet become pregnant.

The words ***Lam yam sasani*** is used in the Koran. This word does not forbid her from legal marriage for her whole life. She or any woman can be touched by the man in future. We can find the same words for women are used ***Lam tamassu honna*** (women had not been touched yet) ---, no Muslim preachers speak about these women as virgins pure in their whole life or forbidden from legal marriage. No Muslim leaders accept this idea. If so, why do they want to use these words to speak about Mary and forbid her from legal marriage? She openly said she is not unchaste (19: 20), meaning that she would have to enter legal marriage to have a child).

But Muslim preachers use the words "***Ruh***" in their explanation of the conception of Jesus in Mary.

Ruh

The Muslim preachers translate the word ***Ruh*** for (1) The Holy Spirit and (2) The Angel. And they used the following verse to cite that Jesus was born from a Virgin mother.

We breathed into her of Our Ruh (21: 91, 66: 12)

This verse translated by the Muslim preachers is totally the same explanation of the crusaders because the Arabic words ***Ruh*** which they translate is The Holy Spirit and they consider that ***Ruh*** is the animated thing (spirit) or life seed which is essential for the living thing to exist. So, in their interpretation "We breathed into her (womb) of Our Spirit."

In this verse, there are two points need to be solved, No. 1 is ***Ruh,*** and No. 2 is ***Fee her***.

In their interpretation of the words ***Fee Her*** as "into her womb", where has the word "womb" come from? There is no such word in original Arabic, ***Fee Her*** means "into her or onto her" and the word "her" refers to the whole body or the whole life, not only mention her womb.

The Holy Koran never says that ***Ruh*** is the Life seed, or the thing which is essential to be the living thing.

And in another interpretation, ***Ruh*** is understood to be Angel.

Both above interpretations come not from the Koran's theory, because the Holy Koran never says that woman is pregnant by Allah's ***Ruh*** or Angel.

And if we follow their interpretation, we get the question of whether Allah blew the Angel into Mary's womb for her to become pregnant. No-Muslim accepts this.

According to the Koran, *Ruh* is not needed to exist living thing.

We can find an example for this in 57:17 "Allah gives life to the earth after his death." This verse clearly describes that non-living thing become the living things because of Allah's permission, without any mention about Ruh. On the other hand, according to this verse, every single living thing exist from the nonliving thing, but the Koran clearly says that only the human being is dignified "***Ruh***" from Allah, which is not dignified to other nonhuman beings. That is why; ***Ruh*** is not the life-seed or sperm to become the living thing. So ***Ruh*** is not needed for the process of pregnancy.

The process of pregnancy

Every human being came out from mother's womb (uterus) and not down from the sky. No where can we find in the Holy Koran that woman is pregnant by Allah's ***Ruh***.

THE INFLUENCE OF ROME

Also, Jesus is a human being who didn't come down from the sky, but came out from his mother's womb, so that her mother cried because of birth pangs when she gave birth to Jesus (19: 23).

The Holy Koran clearly says that "He (Allah) has created you (mankind) from dust, then from a sperm-drop, then from a Leech-like clot, then does He get you out as a child" (40:67). "He (human) is created from a drop-emitted," (86:6). "From a sperm-drop when lodged" (53:46). Allah never creates the man from Angel.

Ruh is not Angel nor dignified to Angel

The pro-Rome-minded Muslim preachers said that **Ruh** refers to the Angel Gabriel, if this were so, according to their interpretation, how was Allah inspired into Mary's womb? (21:91, 66:12) Do they want to say that Allah inspired Angel Gabriel into Mary's womb to get the child (Jesus)? This is very absurd. The Holy Koran contains the word Gabriel three times (2: 97, 8 and 66:4) and nowhere do we find that Gabriel is **Ruh**.

The Angels are not dignified as **Ruh** from Allah, which is why they must prostrate to the human being who is dignified the **Ruh** (15: 30).

According to the Muslim preachers if Gabriel is the Angel, how is he himself the **Ruh**? He himself must obey the human being. The highest power of the Angel is he who carries the **Ruh** to mankind from Allah, (the messenger). (16: 2).

What is *Ruh*?

"The **Ruh** is command of Allah's knowledge it is only a little that is communicated to mankind" (17: 85) this means Allah dignify a very little from His **Ruh** (Knowledge) to mankind.

On the other word, knowledge is carried by the intellect power, so the Holy Koran gives the first meaning for **Ruh** is Intellect or wisdom power that is dignified to mankind when he/she was fashioned completely, not in the step of embryo. (32: 9)

The **Ruh** is dignified to the human being and that's why he/she understands, comprehends, and feels. Otherwise, they are like cattle. The cattle they have eyes, but they see not, they have heard but they hear not, they have heart, but they understand not (7: 179), because they are not dignified the **Ruh**.

The second meaning for the **Ruh** is Allah's selected person or those who have been given the specific wisdom or omen or revelation. Therefore, the human being Jesus is called **Ruhullah** (Allah's **Ruh**). No Muslim preacher defines **Ruhullah** (Jesus) as an Angel.

If so why they do want not define the man clearly (***ba sha ram Sa wee yam***), the messenger of Allah, who gave the pure child to Mary as an Angel (19: 17-19)? That they put on Roman shoes is clear.

The reason that they use is "Surely the likeness of Jesus is with Allah as the likeness of Adam" (3:58). They said that Adam did not have parents and that he came from heaven to world. If Allah wish, Allah can do everything, Allah creates Adam without parent and creates Jesus without father. Their explanation is very absurd; because the verse of Koran (3:58) said the likeness of Jesus is likeness of Adam. Not the likeness of Jesus is half likeness of Adam. When they cite only some parts of this verse and explain to their followers, they used to omit "He created him from dust" and they cite only Jesus is likeness of Adam, and Allah said "Be" so if "Jesus was". They want their followers to accept that Adam is the first person of the world and that he came down from heaven (sky); he had no parents and so on. But the Holy Koran never says that Adam is the first person of the world and came down from heaven (sky). The Holy Koran never says that Adam is created without parent. This verse says clearly that Adam is created from **dust** (on earth not from sky) like every human is created from **dust** (22: 5, 30: 20) same as Jesus and Adam. The whole verse is

"Surely the likeness of Jesus is with Allah as the likeness of Adam; He created him from **dust**, then said to him, Be, and he is going to be." (3: 58)

And from this verse the words ***kun fa ya kuna*** is needed to explain.

"*kun fa ya kuna*"

And then they lure themselves that "***kun fa ya***" means when Allah said "Be" and "Jesus was (immediately) like magic." They cover up about the conception from Mary from 19: 16-22.

In the words "***kun fa ya kuna***", according to the Arabic grammar the prefix word ***Fa*** means "and then", "after that" that means not for past but for future, and the prefix ***Ya*** for future too. These prefixes show that when Allah said "Be" "it is going to be (surely)." "Is going to be" means step by step according to the law of process of nature rather than immediately.

How Mary got pregnant?

Before we go to how Mary got pregnant, we need to heed the following verses.

Allah clearly declares that "Cannot have a child without consult" (6: 102). If someone alters Allah's creation he is ordered by the devil (Satan) 4: 119.

In the Holly Koran Chapter (19)

(16) And mention Mary in the Book when she withdrew in seclusion from her family to an eastern place-

(17) She placed a screen from them; then We sent to Our **Ruh**, and it is a perfect men like her.

(18) She said: Surely, I seek refuge with the most gracious God from you, if you are one guarding (against evil).

(19) He said: I am only a messenger of your Lord: that I will give you a pure boy.

(20) She said: When shall I have a boy and no mortal (man) has touched me nor have I been unchaste?[2]

(21) He said: Even so your Lord says: It is easy to Me: and that We may make him a sign to men and a mercy from Us;[3] and it is a matter which has been decreed.

(22) So, she conceived him; then withdrew herself with him to a remote place.

These verses are from the Koran not from the Myth, when we consider these verses, we can get the clear answer of how Mary conceived. This document says that when Mary left her family and went to eastern place, she found the man like her (spiritual level) who is a messenger of God, **Ruh** (not angel) pure human being; and he gave her a pure boy (pregnant).

---

2 See 'no man touched her'
3 See "Sign to men and mercy from Allah"

But we sorrowfully found that many of commentators transform these clear verses into myth.

They make the **Ruh** from verse 17 as Angel Gabriel who had transformed into human being.

We can say this idea come from Rome's stories not from the Koran, because the Koran never says that the perfect man (well-made man) is created from an Angel, the Koran says that man is created from dust and from parents.[4]

And then we should consider that if **Ruh** in this verse is an Angel, why did she say that; Surely, I seek refuge with the most gracious God from you, if you are one guarding (against evil) in the following verse? When Angel came to her with the message about her son in 3: 45, she did not say these words.

The answer is clearly that in 3:45 -47 the Angel came to her sent news about her son, but in here 19: 17 -22 the messenger who came to her is human being **Bashar** not Angel and he gave her a pure son and not news. How the man gives the child to woman is understood so that she warned to him to guard against evil or follow the law of God because she is not an unchaste woman.

We get one more question in here.

How did the man give the child to her?

Did he bring the child from somewhere and deliver it to her? Or did he rub her womb to get her pregnant? Or did he utter the mystic words to get her pregnant?

The Holly Koran never accepts this kind of myth. According to the Koran, the man can give the child (pregnant) to woman by sexual relation (7:189) or male sperm is essential to female to be conceived. This is law which is prescribed by Allah "The nature made by Allah in which He made men; there is no altering of Allah's creation: that is right religion, ----- (30:30).

The Holy Koran never approved that the child is born because of being sired by Angel or given by Angel.

---

4 See "process of pregnancy"

If the Muslim religious leaders, study the logic (*Mantic*) in their Maddarasa (religious school) and they study the Koran, why do they follow the myth beyond the Koran?

Did Allah reveal the verses of Koran carelessly?

As the Muslim religious leaders change the verses of Koran into myth and translate their bias and deep creed wishes, we should ask them whether Allah revealed the verses of Koran carelessly. We can find clearly in the verses that there is mention of 17 Prophets including Jesus and the pronoun **their** which refers to all of these 17 Prophets, is used as **their fathers, their descendants** and **their brethren** (6: 85-88).

No Muslim dares to say that Allah reveals the verses of Koran carelessly, and the Holly Koran declares itself "We have not neglected anything in the Book" (6:38).

So, the well-trained Muslim leaders try to add the words "**except Jesus**" from the 17 Prophets mentioning the 6:85-87 by using various Arabic grammar omitting Jesus when they interpret the pronoun "**their**" to betray the followers. In these verses, even though there is no word **except Jesus,** why do they want to mislead people with dishonesty?

The answer is clear because they are really followers of Rome.

Overall, our new generation should let our brain be fresh, clear, and we should try to escape from a bewitched, scapegoat.

A sign to men and mercy from Allah

The well-trained Muslim leaders exaggerate the words "a sign to men and mercy from Allah" and use it to try and prove that Jesus was born from a virgin mother because of Allah's *Ruh*, and that Allah makes him a sign to men, and he is called mercy from Allah.

This exaggeration is beyond the Koran. In the Koran Jesus himself said that I have come to you with a sign from your Lord, that I exist to you out of dust like the form of a bird, then I breathed into it and it became a bird, with Allah's permission, and I heal the blind and the leprous, and bring the death to life… (3: 48).

This verse clearly says that "a sign to men" does not mean virgin's son; it means he can do something more than ordinary people can do with Allah' permission.

There may be a little need to explain the words "I exist to you out of dust like the form of a bird, then I breathe into it and it became a bird, with Allah's permission," because some Imams make the story of these words again that Jesus is Virgin's son so he get the mystic power from Allah and he can make the bird toy from dust and breathe into it so it becomes a bird alive.

It is wrong.

The Holly Koran very often uses the metaphor of an animal for the human being. For bad people, bad animals are used as metaphor (2:65, 5:60, 7:179, 25:44, 62:5), and those people who soar to the higher spiritual region and are not bound to earth or earthly thing are called birds (6:38).

The form of a bird from this verse represents the human being. The word "dust" from this verse is clearly poof for it (man is created the dust). Jesus led him to become a higher spiritual person with Allah's permission. Or the prospected spiritual arose people are inspired (instigated) by Jesus to become the holy people with Allah's permission. It does not mean that Jesus can bring the non-lining thing to be alive. He was not a magician; he was a Prophet of God.

And, neither the words "I heal the blind and the leprous" not "bring the death to life" refer to him as a virgin's son.

The Holly Koran does not mean a loss of physical sight when it uses the word "blind" but refers to the loss of spiritual power in a people. (2:7, 18) The disease (leprous) means the same thing happened in their hearts (10:57). Jesus is a Prophet of God, so he teaches the people with the God's permission or God's revelation. It is said he healed the people with disease or blindness, or he brought the dead to life. The Holy Koran itself is the revelation of God; it called itself the teaching which gives the life (8: 24). Nobody, including Jesus can bring the (real) dead to life (23:100).

He shall speak to the people when in the cradle and when of old age. (3:45)

Many Muslim leaders use one part of this verse "speak to the people when in the cradle" and exaggerate about Jesus being a virgin's son so that he can speak to people from when he was very newborn. They used to cover up the part of verse "and when of old age."

This verse is very far from their drawing a conclusion of "virgin's son" from it. In truth, this verse is very against their ideas of Jesus as a character of myth, because this verse clearly states that Jesus was born naturally, and he was growing up step by step from newborn to infant to old age like other healthy men and was not created as a man immediately like magic.

That Jesus started to speak to people from the time when he was in cradle is not any abnormal mystic power because every healthy child of the world starts to speak to people when he/she is in the cradle.

Many Muslim leaders are not followers of the Koran

Even though the Koran proves that it is very pure, straight and reveals the logical law, the Muslim leaders will not surrender their faiths and they try to dispute the Koran which they say they believe in. They follow the myths rather than Koran and narrate those myths to their followers.

Today, although the people are educated, have knowledge, and develop their physical appearance, most of them dare not dispute their myths.

They follow the good narrators (storyteller), and they feel that if they don't accept these myths, they are not the good followers of their religions.

However, even though they have attained the physical development, their brains are still in jail because Rome has caught them and sentenced them forever.

Htay Lwin Oo

Citation

Burmese Books

Bahas Shati Ze war (Mou la na shif ali hta na vi)
Bible (by Rev. A Judson, D. D.)
Dagon University annual magazine (2000)
Guide to the New Testament (by Zaw Thu Lin)
Koran (translated by U Ba Sein)
Koran (commentary of Gazi Mahammad Hashin)
Myat Mingalar Buddhist religious journal (No. 6, 7 Volume 9)
Pitakat (The main scripture of Busddhism)
Zi nat hti pa ka tha ni (by kyi the lay htut Saya daw)

English

Good News Bible (Today's English Version -1991)
Bible (King James Version)
Quran, holy (A group of Muslim brotherhood, Iran)
Qur-an, the holy (Commentary of Maulvi Muhammad Ali)
Qu'ran, the noble (translated by Dr. Muhammad Taqi-ud-Din al Hilali and Dr. Muhammad Muhsin Khan)

Arabic

The Koran

Dictionaries

Burmese- English (Department of literature of Burmese)
Arabic- English (Cosmo Student's dictionary of--- I.G.Hava)
Arabic- English, English- Arabic (Munir Baalbaki)

www.ingramcontent.com/pod-product-compliance
Lightning Source LLC
LaVergne TN
LVHW041552060526
838200LV00037B/1257